theology

Return from a
Distant Country

theology MY

Alister McGrath

Return from a Distant Country

Fortress Press

Minneapolis

RETURN FROM A DISTANT COUNTRY

Originally published by Darton, Longman, and Todd London, UK

Print ISBN: 9781506484341
eBook ISBN: 9781506484358

Cover design: Kristin Miller

Contents

1

Returning from the Distant Country: On Becoming a Theologian

I NEVER EXPECTED to be a Christian theologian, mainly because I never expected to be a Christian. In February 1953, when I was a few weeks old, I was baptized into the Church of Ireland in Down Cathedral, built next to the grave of Patrick, the patron saint of Ireland. By the time I won a scholarship to study the natural sciences at Oxford University some eighteen years later, I had long since migrated to a 'distant country' (Luke 15:13) – an empire of the mind shaped by the converging influences of 1960s Marxism and an aggressive scientism, which held that nothing could be known beyond the natural sciences, for the simple reason that there was nothing beyond them to be known. I assumed that this scientific atheism would be my permanent intellectual homeland; in fact, it turned out to be a temporary place of exile,

9

from which I would later return, wiser and somewhat chastened.[1]

The University of Oxford is central to my story. It was here that my youthful love of the natural sciences was consolidated, given intellectual rigour and depth by those who taught me and supervised my research. I began by taking an undergraduate degree in chemistry, specializing in quantum theory, and then earned an Oxford doctorate for my research in molecular biophysics, working with Professor Sir George Radda in Oxford's Department of Biochemistry. But by then, I had changed. I still loved the sciences; they were, however, now supplemented by a growing sense of the intellectual and imaginative depth of a rediscovered Christianity. I now became focussed on the question of how these two could be brought together, and plausibly held together.

[1] I provide a detailed account of my transition from atheism to Christianity and my initiation into the mysteries of Christian theology in Alister McGrath, *Through a Glass Darkly: Journeys through Science, Faith, and Doubt* (London: Hodder & Stoughton, 2020).

I had arrived at Oxford in October 1971, increasingly aware that my early scientific atheism, though aggressively asserted, was correspondingly inadequately evidenced. I had once seen Marxism as a grand theory, a way of making sense of everything which explained away religion as an outcome of human alienation. Yet reading Karl Popper during the early months of 1971 had raised some difficult issues about both scientific positivism and Marxism. Although I continued to see Marxism as illuminating some aspects of social reality – such as the implications of the fact that we are historically situated – I no longer saw it as offering a totalizing account of reality. Yet Marxism had expanded my mind, creating an intellectual appetite for 'Big Pictures' of reality. I found myself idly wondering whether I would find another that might be more satisfactory.

I had hoped that my growing doubts about atheism would be resolved at Oxford. In fact, they were merely intensified through long conversations with academics and fellow students, as a result of which I came to appreciate the limits placed on human reasoning, and began to grasp for the first time the intellectual capaciousness of Christianity. I never lost my love for the natural sciences, and the methods it had developed for investigating and representing our complex world. Nor did I lose sight of the Marxist insight into the importance of social and historical location in shaping human thought. These insights, acquired during my period of sojourn in a 'distant country', have helped shape my theological agenda and method. Like Augustine of Hippo before me, I now regard these as being like the treasure that the people of Israel took with them as they fled from Egypt, to resource their wayfaring and mould their true identity as they journeyed through the wilderness to the Promised Land.

I began to read C. S. Lewis in February 1974, and soon became aware that his seemingly simple reflections on faith rested on a deep intellectual and imaginative assimilation of the Christian tradition, acquired over decades. Lewis became my gateway to this tradition, creating a longing on my part to immerse myself in Christian theology, so that I might grasp what he had seen before me. I could, however, see no way of studying theology formally at the level which this required. Then, in the first year of my doctoral research in molecular biophysics, I was awarded a Senior Scholarship at Merton College, Oxford, and discovered its terms of reference could allow me to continue my scientific research, while at the same time studying for an undergraduate degree in theology. By the summer of 1978, I had gained my doctorate in molecular biophysics, first class honours in theology, and a complete set of Karl Barth's *Church Dogmatics*, purchased with a generous Denyer and Johnson Prize in Theology, awarded by the university for the best theology degree that year.

I cannot emphasize adequately the importance of this period in shaping my grasp of theology. I was a scientist, steeped in an empirical methodology, who was suddenly plunged into a strange new intellectual world governed by methods and assumptions that never seemed entirely clear. Had I studied these and other aspects of theology on my own, I would probably have floundered. I would have been unable to fully comprehend and assimilate the articles and books I was reading, or realize when I had misunderstood someone or something. But Oxford's traditional tutorial system meant that I was being taught individually by leading scholars, including John Barton (Old Testament), Paul Fiddes (Systematic Theology), Andrew Louth (Patristics), Robert Morgan (New Testament), and Edward Yarnold (medieval theology). My good questions found better answers, and my misunderstandings were graciously corrected.

I now felt I was ready to begin serious advanced study of theology. But what form would this take? Noting that two major contemporary theologians who I studied under Paul Fiddes – Jürgen Moltmann and Wolfhart Pannenberg – began their academic careers with impressively detailed historical studies of earlier theologians, I decided I would do the same. In 1978, I moved to Cambridge University for two years, having been awarded the Naden Studentship for Research in Divinity at St John's College, Cambridge. I began to research the gradual emergence of the ideas of the German theologian Martin Luther in their late medieval context, under the supervision of Professor Gordon Rupp, then Britain's leading authority on Luther, who had just retired as Dixie Professor of Ecclesiastical History at Cambridge. At the same time, I began to prepare for ministry in the Church of England, seeing my future as a theologian lying in some combination of academic and pastoral roles.

My work with Gordon Rupp proved fascinating, and it mushroomed into three interconnected lines of historico-theological research over the next nine years. The original project, which looked at how Luther's distinctive doctrine of justification gradually emerged over the period 1509–19, led me to plan a rather more ambitious engagement with the development of this doctrine from its origins in ancient Israel to the present day, something that had not been attempted since Albrecht Ritschl's pioneering study of 1870. This flowed naturally into a study in the emergence of the theologies of the sixteenth-century Reformation, focussing on the diverse theological methods deployed within this movement, set against the context of the intellectual methodologies of the late Middle Ages and Renaissance.

I returned to Oxford in 1983 as lecturer in Christian doctrine at Wycliffe Hall, a theological college of the Church of England with close links to Oxford University, and quickly became involved in the research and teaching of the Faculty of Theology. This gave me the time and access to library facilities needed to complete these three projects, which were published as *Luther's Theology of the Cross* (1985), *Iustitia Dei: A History of the Christian Doctrine of Justification* (1986), and *The Intellectual Origins of the European Reformation* (1987). I continued developing this solid foundation in historical theology, giving the 1990 Bampton Lectures at Oxford on some issues in this field, and becoming Oxford University's Professor of Historical Theology in 1999.

Yet my real interest lay in engaging the interdisciplinary field of science and religion, which I considered to require both a detailed immersion in a scientific research culture, and a thorough familiarity with the history and development of Christian theology. By 1995, I felt I had a good enough knowledge base to begin work in this field, and tentatively mapped out lines of approach that I felt might be productive, including those assembled in the three volumes of *A Scientific Theology* (2001–3). This exploratory work considered possible lines of engagement and interaction between science and theology, grouped around the main topics of 'Nature,' 'Reality,' and 'Theory'. It was quite clear to me that there were significant ways in which this interaction could be productive, both theologically and apologetically.

I need to stress the apologetic

17

importance of studying the relation of science and theology. In 2002, I took part in a three-way private debate at Balliol College on the rationality of religious belief in the light of the natural sciences. My two atheist opponents in this debate were Peter Atkins, an Oxford physical chemist (who incidentally had earlier taught me quantum theory) and Richard Dawkins, an Oxford evolutionary biologist.

This debate convinced me that there was an urgent need to engage the field of science and religion, as I was now certain that an increasingly important public debate on the rationality of faith was in the process of emerging, with the natural sciences as the chosen weapon of its opponents. Since it was clear to me that Dawkins would be a major voice in this debate, I researched his writings carefully and thoroughly, and shortly afterwards published *Dawkins' God* (2004), the first major critical scholarly account of his understanding of the relation of science and religious faith.

I was right. Two years later, the 'New Atheism' made its noisy appearance, creating massive media interest in questions of religious faith on account of its aggressive rhetoric, its simplistic slogans about religious irrationality, and its vague promissory notes of the end of religion. It was clearly what many wanted to hear, in the light of rising public disquiet about the implications of religious extremism in the wake of 9/11.

The opening salvo was Daniel Dennett's *Breaking the Spell* (2006), which offered a decidedly under-evidenced naturalist account of religion which he apparently believed marked the first occasion on which anyone had thought scientifically about religion. I debated the core ideas of this book with Dennett in London in March 2006 at the Royal Society of Arts. My talk, entitled 'The Spell of the Meme', argued that Dennett rightly raised some interesting critical questions – but did not turn them against his own position, which he seemed to think was exempt from these concerns. I thought otherwise, and highlighted his inconsistent use of the 'meme' in his argument. It soon became clear this epistemic asymmetry was a hallmark of the 'New Atheism': Dennett and Dawkins both failed to judge themselves by the criteria they used to judge others.

A few months later, Dawkins published his *God Delusion*, which became one of the most influential books of the year. After debating Dawkins' views with him on BBC Television that summer, I realized a Christian response was needed, which called into question Dawkins's understanding of both the natural sciences and religion. Knowing his views on these matters better than anyone else, it was not difficult for me to write such a book, focussing on the arguments he set out in *The God Delusion*. In February 2007, four months after I began to write the work, I published *The Dawkins Delusion?*, which became an international bestseller. Other more detailed and considered responses from religious writers followed; this book, however, laid down the core lines of debate.

It lacked the detail and depth to be found later in Rudolf Langthaler's magisterial intervention of 2015,[2] but it was what was urgently needed at the time: a short, clear, and convincing response to Dawkins's core lines of argument.

Public engagement now became a major theme of my writings and lectures. I found that my public lectures on science and faith attracted very large audiences, and allowed me to engage theological questions that were now clearly seen as relevant and important within a wider culture, beyond the traditional academic world. Academically, I began to work on the field of 'natural theology' – a family of ways of understanding how the natural world might disclose or signpost God – and was astonished at the level of interest this created. My 2008 Riddell Memorial Lectures at the University of Newcastle-upon-Tyne, 2009 Gifford Lectures at the University of Aberdeen, and 2009–10 Hulsean

2   Rudolf Langthaler, *Warum Dawkins Unrecht hat: Eine Streitschrift* (Freiburg: Verlag Karl Alber, 2015).

Lectures at the University of Cambridge all focused on this topic. My interest in this field remains, although I am now more interested in exploring how a 'natural philosophy' can serve as an interface between science, philosophy, theology, and personal character formation.

One of the questions that preoccupied me at this time was how Christian clergy could be prepared to deal with such debates about the rationality of religious belief, which were obviously impacting on their congregations. Unpersuaded that the Church of England was taking this question seriously, I left Oxford in 2008 to take up the Professorship of Theology, Ministry, and Education at King's College London. This position allowed me to interact with many clergy across denominations who were studying part-time at King's College to deepen their understanding of their faith, and explore questions of apologetics – a topic on which I was now writing and speaking extensively. It was deeply rewarding to be able to teach students who already knew that these issues were important to their ministries. I was also able to engage in major public discussions of these themes in London, including some significant events at St Paul's Cathedral and Westminster Abbey.

Finally, I returned to Oxford University in April 2014 to take up the Andreas Idreos Professorship of Science and Religion. This provided me with a platform for developing my ideas about the relation of science and theology, while also exploring a broader and perhaps more significant academic theme – the need for theology to engage with other disciplines. I also served as the Gresham Professor of Divinity from 2015–18. This public professorship, established at Gresham College London in 1597, allowed me to continue my work of public engagement, and attracted large audiences. I shall retire from the Idreos chair in September 2022, although I hope to continue to be part of Oxford's outstanding intellectual research culture in some way in the future.

So what are the core theological themes that have excited me, and which I explore in my writings, teaching, and public lectures? In later chapters, I shall reflect on four major themes of my theological vision. I begin, however, by sketching my overall understanding of the nature and purpose of theology.

2

The Eye of the Heart:
Theology as Re-Imagining
the World

THERE IS NO 'right' definition of either theology or a theologian; both terms designate a spectrum of possibilities and responsibilities. For me, theology is a reflective inhabitation of the Christian faith, rooted primarily in the Bible and the long tradition of faithful engagement with this text, and the practice of worship and prayer. Like C. S. Lewis before me, I define myself primarily as a *Christian* theologian, rather than aligning myself with some specific denomination, tradition, or school of thought. I dislike those who use theology primarily to create and sustain divisions within Christianity, when there is so much that may be affirmed in common.

I see theology as the rational and imaginative outcome of Paul's injunction not to conform to the world's ways of thinking, but to be 'transformed through the renewal of

[our] minds' (Romans 12:2). The Greek term *metanoia*, though traditionally (and unhelpfully) translated into English as 'repentance,' is better understood as a 'mental reorientation,' in which we come to understand and imagine reality in a new way. Christianity demands discipleship, including a 'discipleship of the mind',[3] which embraces – but is not limited to – what we call 'theology'. I take with the greatest seriousness Christ's summary of the First Commandment, which calls for us to love God with our minds, as well as our hearts (Mark 12:30). I have also reflected carefully about Paul's reference to believers possessing 'the mind of Christ' (1 Corinthians 2:16), a phrase which suggests a settled way of thinking and understanding that is shaped by the Christian faith.

My views on the nature and tasks of theology began to emerge as I studied early Christian theologians (then generally referred

[3]   I frequently engage this theme: see, for example, Alister McGrath, *Mere Discipleship: On Growing in Wisdom and Hope* (London: SPCK, 2018)·

to as 'patristic writers') at Oxford back in 1977 under Andrew Louth. As I wrestled with Irenaeus of Lyons, Athanasius of Alexandria, and Augustine of Hippo, I began to see patterns emerging. Theology seemed to be about achieving a synthesis of the Christian faith, which involved weaving together biblical texts to create a coherent way of seeing the world.

Back in the 1970s, the idea of 'inference to the best explanation' was beginning to gain traction within the scientific community, displacing older approaches to scientific explanation, such as Carl Hempel's 'Deductive-Nomological Model.' This new approach began from the traditional Aristotelian idea of 'preserving the phenomena,' and moved on to consider how well various theories were able to weave these observations together into a coherent whole. The 'best' theory was the one that seemed to achieve the most compelling synthesis of these phenomena, in the judgement of the scientific community.

I could see an obvious connection with

theology. Drawing on Aristotle's notion of the *bios theōretikos*, I began to see theology as a *theōria*, a way of 'beholding' or 'contemplating' reality which sought to bring together and hold together coherently the complex biblical witness to the nature of God, and the identity and significance of Jesus Christ. The many elements of the biblical witness were the 'phenomena'; theology was the theoretical framework that integrated them into a coherent whole. I have little time for 'proof-texting' – the citation of a single biblical text to resolve complex issues. The task of theology is to find the 'Big Picture' which weaves together individual biblical texts and themes coherently and credibly, rather than allow any individual text to be taken as normative in isolation.

My teenage experimentations with Marxism led me to experience the imaginative excitement associated with 'Big Picture' thinking. For a while, Marxism became the theoretical lens through which I viewed history and experience, before my reading of Karl Popper made me aware of its limitations.

Yet devouring C. S. Lewis's essay 'Is Theology Poetry' in February 1974 was like a moment of intellectual illumination, in which I suddenly realized that Christianity could also be seen as offering such a 'Big Picture,' which could be conceptually and imaginatively comprehensive without being intellectually imperialist. The conclusion to that essay has remained in my mind and shaped my thinking to this day: 'I believe in Christianity as I believe that the Sun has risen, not only because I see it, but because by it I see everything else.'[4]

I thus see theology as discerning and exploring the 'Big Picture' of the Christian faith which is disclosed in the Christian Bible, and the long Christian tradition of wrestling with this text. As I read early Christian writers, I noticed that they were deeply rooted in the Bible, yet were able to articulate its insights in such a way that they opened up and allow us to inhabit a wider and deeper vision of

[4]   C. S. Lewis, *They asked for a Paper* (London: Bles, 1962), 165. I later found a similar approach in other writers – such as Dante and G. K. Chesterton.

reality. Theology is biblical; yet it is *more than biblical,* in that it seeks to weave biblical themes together and discern the richer picture which results – a picture which cannot be fully disclosed by a single biblical passage. If biblical themes are the threads, the theology is the tapestry that results from weaving them together. If individual biblical passages are brush strokes, then theology is the picture which they disclose.

Most of the early Christian doctrinal debates – such as the Arian controversy of the fourth century, and the Pelagian controversy of the fifth century – could easily be framed in terms of achieving the best synthesis of the biblical witness, using criteria which paralleled, but were not identical to, those now used in scientific explanation – such as coherence and comprehensiveness. Athanasius used the criterion of coherence during the Arian controversy, for example, arguing that Arius's Christology offered a conceptually incoherent account of salvation. Yet Athanasius also appealed to the criterion of the Christian practice of worship, seeing this as something handed down from the apostles which embedded and enacted some implicit yet definitive theological themes. Arius's Christology, Athanasius insisted, was simply not consistent with this practice.

Now let me concede immediately that this view of theology would not command universal assent. However, it is the way in which I have come to see its identity and role. I find it reflected in Augustine of Hippo's programmatic statement in *Sermon 88*, in which he declares that the Christian faith is about 'healing the eye of the heart (*sanare oculum cordis*)' so that that God can be seen properly. Yet while I affirm the capacity of Christian theology to illuminate reality, I must stress that it does not, and cannot, achieve a total clarity of vision in this life. There are parallels here with the biblical descriptions of Moses approaching God, who is portrayed as shrouded in cloud and darkness (e.g. Deuteronomy 5:22). Theology is about wrestling with the living God, who overwhelms our capacity to understand and to depict – an idea many theologians see echoed in the biblical account of Jacob retiring wounded from wrestling with an angel at Penuel (Genesis 32:22–32).

I thus gladly embrace the term 'mystery' to speak about God and Christ – not because my faith is irrational, but because my limited capacities as a human being mean that I cannot hope to grasp these realities fully. As the Franciscan theologian Thomas Weinandy, who I knew when he was based in Oxford, once remarked: 'Because God, who can never be fully comprehended, lies at the heart of all theological enquiry, theology by its nature is not a *problem solving* enterprise, but rather a *mystery discerning* enterprise.'[5] There is much wisdom in those words.

Finally, I need to say something about how I understand the place of a theologian. I believe that theology is called to engage three main audiences – the academy, the churches,

[5] Thomas G. Weinandy, *Does God Suffer?* (Notre Dame, IN: University of Notre Dame Press, 2000), 32 [my emphasis].

and culture at large. I am located within the academy, and value its intellectual freedom, its love of learning, and the wisdom of my professional colleagues. Yet I also stand *within* – not above or outside – the Christian community of faith. I try to serve that community by helping it to appreciate and benefit from its rich intellectual and spiritual heritage, while also recognizing the importance of speaking to a wider culture on behalf of that community of faith about what it believes, and why this is to be taken seriously.

Thus far, I have tended to speak about theology in rather unfocussed general terms. In the chapters which follow, I shall briefly explore my views on the four main themes that have dominated my own theology, several of which reflect questions arising from my personal journey of faith and development. Each is linked with academic positions I have held during my career, and specific audiences I have engaged.

1. I was Professor of Historical Theology at Oxford University from 1999 to 2008. In

Chapter 3, I will reflect on the significance of historical theology for articulating Christian theology in the present.

2. I held the Andreas Idreos Professorship of Science and Religion at Oxford University from 2014 to 2022. In Chapter 4, I will set out my ideas on the importance of interdisciplinarity in general, and the specific significance of the natural sciences for Christian theology.

3. I served as the Gresham Professor of Divinity in the City of London from 2015 to 2018. This Professorship was established in 1597 at Gresham College, to encourage wider public engagement with theological issues. In Chapter 5, I shall explain my views on public theological engagement, and the growing role for Christian apologetics in the life of the churches.

4. I taught at Wycliffe Hall, Oxford – a leading theological college of the Church

of England – for more than twenty years, before becoming Professor of Theology, Ministry and Education at King's College London from 2008 to 2014. In Chapter 6, I shall explain why I consider theological education to be so important, and how it fits into my overall vision of myself as a theologian.

3

Immersed in the Tradition: Historical Theology

DURING THE FIRST part of my career as a theologian, I focussed on historical theology, seeing this both as a valuable end in itself, and at the same time as an essential preliminary to theological engagement with present-day concerns. So what is historical theology? Though often misunderstood simply as the study of the history of theology, historical theology is actually about grasping how theology has been done *in a specific historical context*. How does this context shape the questions that are asked, and the answers that are given?

Although I had lost faith in Marxism as a totalizing worldview by this stage, I remained acutely appreciative of its usefulness as a tool of historical analysis, and maintained contact with writers in this tradition. For example, I formed an intellectual friendship with the

Polish Marxist philosopher and intellectual historian Leszek Kołakowski, author of the magisterial *Main Currents of Marxism,* who settled in Oxford after being thrown out of Poland for publicly criticizing Marxist orthodoxy. I organized an international symposium on his work at Oxford in October 2007 to celebrate his 80th birthday.

So what insights might Marxism bring to historical theology? Here's one. Marx's comment of 1852 cannot be overlooked by any serious theologian: 'People make their own history, but they do not make it as they please under circumstances of their own choosing, but under circumstances that already exist, given and handed down to them.'[6] Marx's point is this: whether we like it or not, we do theology within an inherited and limiting historical context, precisely because we are *culturally and historically embedded*. Our historicity limits our options.

Theology cannot avoid being influenced

[6]   Karl Marx, *Der achtzehnte Brumaire des Louis Bonaparte*, 2nd ed. (Hamburg: Otto Meissner, 1869),

by the historical context within which it is undertaken. Historical theology may be primarily concerned with the *history* of theology at any given point; yet it is secondarily about understanding how the challenges, assumptions, and resources of that historical moment *shaped and limited* those theological formulations.

The theologian of today can benefit from the riches of the theological tradition; yet this tradition clearly needs to be interpreted rather than simply restated, on account of the disparity between its original context and its present equivalent. I later found this point expressed rather well by Emil Brunner: 'There is indeed an *evangelium perennis* but not a *theologia perennis* . . . The gospel remains the same, but our understanding of the gospel must ever be won anew.'[7] My substantial intellectual investment in historical theology was thus not a nostalgic retreat into the past to escape the present; it was learning how things

[7] Emil Brunner, 'Toward a Missionary Theology' (*Christian Century* 66, no. 27 (1949): 816–18; quote at 816).

had been done in the past, to help me do them better in the present. The challenge is to *frame* the truths of faith in today's languages and concepts, without *trapping* the gospel within those languages and concepts.

Historical theology taught me that most of today's theological questions were asked – and answered – in the past. New questions do need engagement, such as those arising from Darwin's theory of natural selection and Einstein's theory of general relativity. Yet it is as if there are a set of questions about God, Christ, and human nature to which we keep returning, hoping to refresh our theological vision and make fresh applications. This led me to realize the value of a deep immersion in the history of theology: it opens up a new world of possibilities for the sympathetic evaluation and retrieval of ideas and approaches that have been prematurely declared to be redundant or outdated.

Now this is not a *new* idea; many sixteenth-century theologians, for example, saw themselves as rediscovering the insights

44

of patristic writers such as Augustine of Hippo and finding new ways of applying them to their own unsettled age. It is, however, a *timely* idea, as it allows us to affirm that we stand within the flux of history, and can learn from what has happened before us without being trapped in the past. It gives us a sense of historical location, so that we can see ourselves as standing within an ongoing tradition of reflection and interpretation, in which some degree of continuity with the past is both assumed and valued. This point is made neatly by C. S. Lewis: 'Humanity does not pass through phases as a train passes through stations: being alive, it has the privilege of always moving yet never leaving anything behind. Whatever we have been, in some sort we are still.'[8] Lewis's remarks help me frame both myself and the theological enterprise in a broader and deeper context.

It is also important to note that some theological developments turn out to be

[8] C. S. Lewis, *The Allegory of Love: A Study in Medieval Tradition* (Cambridge: Cambridge University Press, 2013), 2.

inappropriate or unhelpful, and thus requiring correcting and redirecting. As I understand it, theology is critical and conservative, in the best senses of both terms, putting everything to the test and holding on to what is good (1 Thessalonians 5:21). This can mean interrogating some theological ideas concerning their foundation and validity. For example, does the classic early Christian idea of the impassibility of God represent an inappropriate accommodation to Hellenistic philosophical prejudices, and thus require reconsideration? As I pointed out in my 1990 Bampton Lectures at Oxford,[9] the discipline of doctrinal criticism remains important in preserving theological integrity, and ensuring that Christian theology is not trapped within or determined by the contingencies of any historical mindset or cultural location.

Yet historical theology can too easily treat theologians as historically-located idea-

[9] Alister E. McGrath, *The Genesis of Doctrine: A Study in the Foundations of Doctrinal Criticism* (Oxford: Blackwell, 1990).

generating machines. Theologians, we must remember, are *human beings*, with passions, aspirations, and concerns. For this reason, I have come to value – and to write! – theological biographies. In exploring the lives of writers such as Emil Brunner, C. S. Lewis, and T. F. Torrance, I have come to understand something of the problems they identified, the solutions they advocated and how they developed them, and the difference this made to them. It is a reminder that theology is an *historically located* and *personally embodied* activity on the one hand, and a *personally transformative* enterprise on the other. Biographies are not about abstract thoughts; they are about *embodied minds that are thinking*.

So how did this ongoing engagement with historical theology shape my theological outlook? There are four points to note here.

1. It helps me to see myself as standing in a long tradition of reception and interpretation of something I discovered, but did not invent.

47

2. It encourages me to learn from those who have wrestled before me with the interpretation of the Bible and the articulation of core themes of the faith.

3. It invites me to see myself as responsible for passing on this heritage to the future, not by passively repeating it, but by actively engaging and developing it.

4. In exploring how the ideas and approaches of other theologians were shaped by their historical location, I have to reflect on how I might myself be the prisoner of my own historical context and my personal history, and how can I hope to transcend this.

I thus see myself as part of a community of exploration, engaged on a shared journey of discovery. We can learn from those who have travelled this road before us. As I see it, I have to work things out from within the flow of history, in dialogue with others who have made that journey before me, and who are now

48

making that journey around me. We have to allow – perhaps even expect – that they may have seen something that we have *failed* to see through inattentiveness, or *refused* to see through prejudice.

Some words of Marcel Proust come to mind here: the 'only true voyage of discovery', he suggested, is 'not to travel to new landscapes, but to possess other eyes, to behold the universe through the eyes of another, of a hundred others.'[10] Perhaps the greatest gift of historical theology is to allow us to see the gospel through the eyes of others, thus enriching and extending our own theological vision.

[10] Marcel Proust, *La prisonnière* (Paris: Gallimard, 1925), 69.

4

Making Connections: Science and Religion

ALL THEOLOGIANS HAVE a personal history,
which to some extent shapes and directs
their theological vision. Several elements
of my own history have played an important
role in shaping my theological agendas. One
is my growing realization that my earlier
embrace of atheism was a result of failing
to understand the nature of Christianity, and
grasp the capaciousness of its intellectual
vision. Another is my lingering intellectual
respect for Marxism, particularly as a tool for
cultural analysis. (I sometimes like to think
of myself in Gramscian terms as an 'organic
theologian'.) Yet perhaps the most important
is my ongoing love for the natural sciences,
which has remained with me throughout my
life. How, I often wondered during the early
1970s, might it be possible to hold the natural

sciences and the Christian faith together?[11]

One intellectual strategy that was popular in Oxford Christian student circles in the early 1970s was to allocate science and faith to different mental compartments. Each was valued, yet they were considered to be compatible yet independent, existing alongside each other in a splendid isolation which was resistant to conceptual clarification. I was not satisfied with this approach, feeling it was essential to develop some form of intellectual framework that would enable me to see my science and faith as parts of a greater whole, rather than disconnected and unrelated intellectual zones. I found a temporary solution to this dilemma in the early 1970s through Charles A. Coulson's idea that science and religion offer multiple perspectives on reality.

Coulson was then Oxford's Professor

---

[11]   For a more detailed account, see Alister E. McGrath, 'Loving Science, Discovering God: An Autobiographical Reflection on Science and Theology', *Theology & Science* 17 (2019): 431–43.

of Theoretical Chemistry and a Methodist local preacher, and I respected both his professional standing as a scientist, and his concern to integrate his faith and science. Coulson offered me a holding position which was perfectly adequate while I explored other possibilities. Over the next thirty years, I assessed multiple frameworks of interpretation which might illuminate this relationship, including Roy Bhaskar's critical realism, Nicolai Hartmann's stratified ontology, Mary Midgley's idea of the multiple mapping of a complex reality, Edgar Morin's *pensée complexe*, Ken Wilber's integral theory, and E. O. Wilson's concept of consilience.[12] In the end, I came to the conclusion that while none of these was capable of universal application, each offered at least some degree of clarification concerning how the natural sciences and Christian theology could be

[12]   For the outcome of this process, see the cautious position outlined in Alister E. McGrath, *The Territories of Human Reason: Science and Theology in an Age of Multiple Rationalities* (Oxford: Oxford University Press, 2019).

seen as elements of a greater vision of human knowledge.

It was clear to me, coming from an interdisciplinary scientific research culture, that Christian theology and different scientific disciplines used different research methods. I found a congenial dialogue partner in exploring this theme in the works of the leading Scottish theologian Thomas F. Torrance, especially his major work *Theological Science* (1969) which I first read in June 1979.[13] Theologically, the question I had to engage was whether using such different research methods led simply to an uncorrelated and unintegrated plurality of outcomes, or whether there was some way of weaving these outcomes together to disclose a coherent greater picture.

Today, after a thorough and extended exploration of the options, I tend to focus in my teaching and public engagement on three

[13] For the importance of this work to my thinking, see Alister E. McGrath, 'A Manifesto for Intellectual Engagement: Reflections on Thomas F. Torrance's *Theological Science* (1969)', *Participatio* 7 (2018): 1–16.

main imaginative representations of the relation and possibilities for correlation of the natural sciences and Christian theology. Each begins from the fundamental recognition of the ontological unity of our complex world, which entails a methodological pluralism in its proper investigation. As these approaches are developed in detail in my more recent works, I shall simply offer some brief comments on each.

1. *Science and theology represent different perspectives on our complex world.* This is the view I was introduced to by Charles Coulson back in the 1970s, and it remains important to me today. Coulson, an enthusiastic mountaineer, illustrated his approach by asking his readers to join him in an imagined walk around the great Scottish mountain Ben Nevis, and to reflect on how the mountain appeared when it was seen viewed from different angles.[14] Each observer gives the best

[14] C. A. Coulson, *Christianity in an Age of Science* (London: Oxford University Press, 1953), 18–34.

account they can of Ben Nevis, as seen from their perspective, and then combines these with the perspectives of other observers. The complex structure of Ben Nevis cannot be grasped fully from any single angle of approach. A full description requires these different perspectives to be brought together, and integrated into a single coherent picture. The whole is the sum of these multiple perspectives; no single perspective can be seen as offering a satisfactory account of the greater whole. It is a simple analogy, and it is easily applied to the relation of science and faith. Yet more needs to be said.

2. *Science and theology engage different levels of our complex world.* This approach recognizes that reality is multi-layered, and that each of these layers needs to be explored in its own distinct way, using a research method adapted to its special characteristics. I came across this way of thinking during the 1990s in the 'critical

realism' of the social philosopher Roy Bhaskar, and I was the first theologian to make active use of his approach.[15] I lectured twice on critical realist approaches to theology at the annual meetings of the International Association for Critical Realism.

For Bhaskar, each individual science deals with a different stratum of reality, and so has to develop and use methods of investigation that are adapted and appropriate to this stratum. Ontology thus determines epistemology. The insights derived from investigating multiple levels of reality in accord with their distinct identities need then to be brought together to give a coherent and comprehensive account of this complex reality. The scientific method thus simply cannot engage theological questions, or displace theology as a discipline.

[15] Brad Shipway, 'The Theological Application of Bhaskar's Stratified Reality: The Scientific Theology of A. E. McGrath', *Journal of Critical Realism* 3 (2004): 191–203.

Scientism improperly assumes, without any compelling evidence, that a method which works well at one level can – and must – be used at every level.

3. *Science and theology offer different maps of our complex world.*

    The philosopher Mary Midgley invites us to think of using 'multiple maps' to do justice to the complexity of reality.[16] Different maps provide different information about the same reality. We need multiple mappings of reality because each such mapping is incomplete, and focusses on some specific question that is being asked. The critical task is to lay these maps over one another, and combine the information that each conveys.

A physical map of North America thus does not make a political map of that same region

[16] For my critical engagement with this approach, see Alister E. McGrath, 'The Owl of Minerva: Reflections on the Theological Significance of Mary Midgley', *Heythrop Journal* 61, no. 5 (2020): 852–64, especially 853–6.

irrelevant, in that we need to map both physical and social realities. Each map is to be respected, but it depends on a specific way of exploring our world, and is incomplete. It needs supplementation with other maps. A scientific map helps us understand how we, as human beings, function – which is important *medically*. Yet a theological map helps us understand our deeper needs – which is important *spiritually*.

It will be clear that, in briefly setting out these three approaches to visualizing the relation of the natural sciences and theology, I am implicitly rejecting two significant and influential approaches to the question, both of which I regard as inadequate in terms of their intellectual foundations and outcomes.

1. *Dialogue is impossible or pointless.* Stephen Jay Gould's concept of 'non-overlapping magisteria (NOMA)' is framed in terms of maintaining and respecting intellectual and professional integrity.[17]

[17] Stephen Jay Gould, 'Nonoverlapping Magisteria', *Natural History* 106 (1997), 16–22.

Yet Gould's intellectual isolationism prematurely closes down some potentially significant conversations, and effectively forces individuals who are both scientists and believers to bifurcate their thinking into Gould's isolated compartments.

2. *Theology (or science) can answer all meaningful questions.* This intellectually colonialist view holds that certain disciplines are superior to others, and are able to answer all of life's fundamental questions. There is therefore no point in consulting other disciplines on such matters. Such claims to epistemic privilege are, unfortunately, especially associated with scientific popularism, such as the simplistic and unevidenced assertion that science has rendered philosophy redundant.[18] For some popular scientific writers, such as Peter Atkins

---

[18] See the hopeless overstatements in Stephen Hawking and Leonard Mlodinow, *The Grand Design* (New York: Bantam Books, 2010).

or Richard Dawkins, philosophical questions are either meaningless, or can be answered far more effectively and reliably by science.

This intellectually imperialist view is often referred to as 'scientism', which can be formally defined as 'a totalizing attitude that regards science as the ultimate standard and arbiter of all interesting questions; or alternatively that seeks to expand the very definition and scope of science to encompass all aspects of human knowledge and understanding.'[19] Scientism has become the undergirding philosophy of the 'New Atheism,' the populist atheist movement that weaponized science in its attempt to discredit and marginalize religion. The movement's intellectual over-reach, which eventually led to its unravelling, was mainly due to its unwise embrace of an aggressive form of scientism which turned out

[19] Massimo Pigliucci, 'New Atheism and the Scientistic Turn in the Atheism Movement', *Midwest Studies in Philosophy* 37, no. 1 (2013): 142–53; quote at 144.

to be vulnerable to charges of superficiality and intellectual circularity.

This leads me to emphasize an important function of Christian theology – the challenging of inadequate secular accounts of nature and humanity. Emil Brunner spoke of the 'other' task of theology,[20] namely the critique or subversion of purely naturalist accounts of humanity and nature. One of the reasons why I have been so interested in 'natural theology' is that it opens up a deeper way of rendering nature which is much more aesthetically and imaginatively engaging than the somewhat emaciated and impoverished account of nature offered by the scientism of Dawkins and others.[21]

While some, overlooking recent scholarship, still speak of an intrinsic and essential conflict between the natural sciences and theology, I prefer to focus on how an appropriate

[20] Emil Brunner, 'Die andere Aufgabe der Theologie' in *Ein offenes Wort: Vorträge und Aufsätze 1917–1962.* 2 vols. Zurich: Theologischer Verlag, 1981, vol. 1, 171–93.
[21] See, for example, Alister E. McGrath, *Re-Imagining Nature: The Promise of a Christian Natural Theology* (Oxford: Wiley-Blackwell, 2016), 156–63.

angle of approach allows us to think of their potential mutual enrichment. I recognize that the natural sciences and Christian theology use quite different methods in their production of knowledge. While dogmatic rationalists assert that this demonstrates that they are *incompatible*, they are in fact merely *different*. In recent years, I have made extensive use of Mary Midgley's notion of multiple intellectual toolkits to cope with the complexity of reality. Midgley sets out this idea as follows:

> No one pattern of thought – not even in physics – is so 'fundamental' that all others will eventually be reduced to it. Instead, for most important questions in human life, a number of different conceptual tool-boxes always have to be used together.[22]

Every intellectual discipline develops its own distinct method of engagement and criteria of

[22] Mary Midgley, 'Dover Beach: Understanding the Pains of Bereavement', *Philosophy* 81, no. 316 (2006): 209–30; quote at 219. Cf. McGrath, 'Owl of Minerva', 853–7.

evaluation, developed specifically to deal with its own area of research. Yet these disciplines may subsequently be brought into conversation with each other, in that their insights, though derived in different manners and relating to different aspects of our world, might lead to an enriched understanding of our world and life as a whole.

Why does this matter? While I personally think that the philosopher John Dewey overstated things when he declared that the 'deepest problem of modern life' is that we have failed to integrate our 'thoughts about the world' with our thoughts about 'value and purpose',[23] I entirely agree with him in recognizing the need to weave together different insights about the world and human existence. To simplify a complex argument, presented in much greater detail in my later writings, science helps us understand how things *work*; theology helps us grasp what things *mean*. We need to hold these together,

[23] John Dewey, *The Quest for Certainty* (New York: Capricorn Books, 1960), 255.

seeing them as integral elements of a 'Big Picture' of reality.

And that, in my view, is what theology helps us to do – to recapture the coherence and unity of our world, which is so easily lost, compromised or obscured by the rise of disciplinary specificity on the one hand, and reductionist approaches to nature on the other.

5

Public Engagement:
The Art of Apologetics

CHRISTIANITY, IN MY view, does not simply proclaim and enable personal and communal transformation; it is about the articulation of a moral, intellectual and spiritual vision with the capacity to capture the imagination and transform the mind of the wider culture. I have never seen theology as a retreat into a private realm of ideas, but rather as establishing the foundation for public engagement, allowing the relevance and vitality of faith to be explored and explained, often in critical dialogue with its cultural alternatives.

My own personal journey of faith has had a significant impact on my understanding of the purpose and place of theology. My teenage atheism arose partly because nobody helped me to see why Christianity was so interesting, or set out possible responses to the criticisms which I levelled against it. Theology, as I understand it, publicly articulates and defends an intellectually and imaginatively compelling vision of reality. In taking this position, I am firmly rejecting both the Pietist tendency to reduce Christianity to a privatized spirituality, and the Fundamentalist inclination to disengage from any serious conversation with secular culture, on account of the alleged risk of intellectual contamination.

Public theological engagement is best undertaken by individual people of faith who can speak personally on behalf of their grand vision of reality, rather than by bishops or church officials, who are inevitably seen as compromised by their institutional precommitments and the moral baggage of institutional history. This public engagement is based upon, but not limited to, three core areas of reflection.

1. Showing that Christianity is able to make sense of reality, leading into the perhaps more significant assertion that it is able to

enable the transformation of personal and communal existence.

2. Engaging critical questions and concerns about faith that are seen to be significant for many in contemporary culture.

3. Offering a criticism of alternative worldviews or dominant philosophies (such as scientism), which often gain cultural ascendency through historical contingencies rather than intellectual necessity (a point stressed by Charles Taylor in his *Secular Age*).

All of these fall within the domain of what is traditionally known as 'Christian Apologetics', which has been an important area of Christian public engagement since the second century.

The rise and fall of the 'New Atheism,' which began in 2006 and fizzled out a decade later, demonstrated the significance of all three of these areas of discussion and debate for Christian theology. I was heavily involved in debates with leading 'New Atheists' in Britain and North America, alongside two other Oxford academics: John Lennox (Professor of Mathematics), and Keith Ward (a former Regius Professor of Divinity). While some theologians treat apologetics somewhat disdainfully as a deplorable recent innovation, I see it as an authentic, traditional, and appropriate enactment of theology, which ultimately rests on a deep immersion in the theological tradition on the one hand, and a familiarity with the concerns of contemporary culture on the other – especially when these are seen as hostile to faith.

In challenging the 'New Atheism', I focused on a number of issues that clearly needed to be engaged, both in terms of contesting the over-statements of some of its leading representatives, and offering an alternative way of seeing things. For example, both Richard Dawkins and Christopher Hitchens are clearly critically dependent on the 'warfare model' of the relation of science and faith in framing their criticisms of the vague generality they call 'religion'. It is easily shown that this model is a social construction of the late Enlightenment, given added cultural significance by the social circumstances of late nineteenth century England. In its place, I offered an 'enrichment' model, which many in those audiences found deeply attractive.

Both Dawkins and his 'New Atheist' colleague Sam Harris also depend excessively on a rather naive scientism in rejecting the need to take seriously moral philosophy or theology. Yet this position, which holds that the natural sciences alone are able to establish truth (pp. 63-4), is easily shown to be intellectually circular, and is ultimately a matter of personal belief rather than proven fact. Now most theologians would assent to both these criticisms. My point, however, is that these criticisms need to be made *publicly*, so that they can be part of a wider discussion. Non-engagement simply leads to the silencing of Christian perspectives in these wider cultural discussions, or entrusting them to amateurs.

For me, apologetics is best seen, not as a vigorous criticism of alternatives to Christian faith, but rather as a positive invitation to step inside the Christian 'Big Picture', and appreciate the quality of its theological rendering of reality and its capacity to make sense of things. Apologetics is an invitation to see things in a new way, which Christianity insists is both true and trustworthy.

Some apologists focus on demonstrating the truth of individual threads of this Christian tapestry of faith, offering detailed justifications of, for example, the existence of God. That is certainly useful — but like G. K. Chesterton before me, I hold that what really matters is the 'Big Picture.' In describing his own return to faith in 1903, Chesterton famously remarked that:

> ... numbers of us have returned to this belief; and that we have returned to it, not because of this argument or that argument, but because the theory, when it is adopted, works out everywhere; because the coat,

when it is tried on, fits in every crease. ... We have returned to it because it is an intelligible picture of the world.[24]

For Chesterton, the appeal of Christianity lies in its internal coherence and external correspondence with the experiential world of ordinary people. That, to me, is why theology is the best foundation for apologetics – and why the best apologetics is a public theology.

[24] *G. K. Chesterton at the Daily News*, ed. Julia Stapleton. 4 vols (London: Pickering & Chatto, 2012), vol. 2, 24–6.

6

Unpacking the Treasure Chest: Theological Education

MY PERSONAL CORRESPONDENCE suggests that I am widely seen, not as a significant original thinker, but as a learned and accessible theological gateway to a rich tradition that needs introducing and explaining. I am widely considered to be a theologian who is particularly good at introducing other theologians, enabling them to be better understood and appreciated. So how did this happen, and how does it fit into my vision of theology?

I began to study Christian theology at Oxford University in 1976. I found it very difficult to make the transition from chemistry to theology. Not only did these two disciplines use quite different methods of inquiry; I also had a huge amount of new information to accumulate and absorb. In the case of chemistry, advanced learning in the field was made easy on account of several excellent textbooks – such as March's *Advanced Organic Chemistry*, and Cotton and Wilkinson's *Advanced Inorganic Chemistry*. There was no theological equivalent back then. I had to learn everything from ground zero.

Happily, Oxford University uses the tutorial system for teaching at undergraduate level, and I was fortunate to have some of Oxford's leading theologians and biblical scholars to introduce me to the field, and help me find my way. With their help, I gradually began to grasp how theology worked, and catch a glimpse of its enormous potential for spiritual enrichment and cultural engagement. When I myself later began to teach theology at Oxford to both university students of theology and students who were preparing for ministry in the Church of England, I had a good sense of both the obstacles that they would face, and how the riches of the Christian theological tradition could be explained and applied.

For a period of twenty years, from 1983 to 2004, I gave an introductory course of lectures on theology at Oxford, and gradually identified and developed approaches to teaching theology that my audiences found accessible, and ways of explaining core theological ideas that they found persuasive. I did not see my role as a teacher in terms of telling my audiences what they should think, but rather as explaining what had been thought, thus allowing them to craft their own understandings of theology.

An Oxford publisher heard of the impact these lectures were having, and asked me to develop them into a textbook. We gave it the unimaginative title *Christian Theology: An Introduction*. It appeared in 1993, is now in its sixth edition, and has been translated into twenty languages. Encouraged by its success, I developed other theological textbooks, including sets of readings with detailed introductions and commentary, aiming to encourage students to engage primary sources, rather than being dependent on secondary studies such as mine.

My textbooks focused on *Christian* theology, drawing on C. S. Lewis's notion of a shared consensual orthodoxy that he termed 'mere Christianity'. Like Lewis before me, I did not see any need to prioritize or limit myself to any specific form of Christianity, but to display the riches of that tradition in its totality. Catholic, evangelical, Orthodox and Protestant contributions were all woven into my narrative, and discussed respectfully and fairly.

The gospel image (Matthew 13:52) of a householder opening up a 'storehouse' or 'treasure chest' (*thesauros)* and 'bringing out new things as well as old' captures something of my approach. Rather than needlessly reinvent wheels, theology can reach into its past and retrieve and reinvigorate ideas so that they can find a new lease of life or fresh application today. Yet the only way of alerting today's theologians to the value of the past *as a present theological resource* is through immersion in the tradition, learning how the Bible was interpreted in the past, and how theological ideas were developed and put into practice.

The past can refresh us. C. S. Lewis made this point well, in his 1944 preface to a translation of Athanasius of Alexandria's *de incarnatione*. To read classic works of theology is to 'keep the clean sea breeze of the centuries blowing through our minds'.[25] We all need such refreshing breezes. Reading other theologians, past and present, enables us to see the Christian faith through other eyes, perhaps discovering something they have seen that can enrich our own vision of faith.

So will I be remembered as a theologian? I doubt it, except perhaps in one sense. Future theologians need will help in getting started – as I did. Maybe my legacy will turn out to be helping young theologians find their feet, so that they can develop their own visions of theology. I'm very happy with that modest thought. It's good to have been useful.

[25] C. S. Lewis, 'On the Reading of Old Books' in *Essay Collection* (London: HarperCollins, 2002), 440.

A Brief Curriculum Vitae

Education

First Class Honours, Final Honour School of Natural Sciences (Chemistry), Oxford University, 1975. Specialist subject: Quantum Theory.

Doctor of Philosophy (DPhil), Oxford University, 1978, for research in molecular biophysics, under the supervision of Professor Sir George Radda, FRS.

First Class Honours, Final Honour School of Theology, Oxford University, 1978. Specialist subjects: science and religion; medieval theology.

Doctor of Divinity (DD), Faculty of Theology, Oxford University, 2001, for research in historical and systematic theology.

Doctor of Letters (DLitt), Division of Humanities, Oxford University, 2013, for research in science and religion, especially natural theology.

Employment

1983–2004 Lecturer in historical and systematic theology, then Principal, Wycliffe Hall, Oxford.

1983–1993 Also member of Faculty of Theology, Oxford University

1993–1999 Also University Research Lecturer in Theology, Oxford University

1999–2008 Also Professor of Historical Theology, Oxford University

2008–2014 Professor of Theology, Ministry and Education, King's College, London.

2014–2022 Andreas Idreos Professor of Science and Religion, Oxford University

2015–18 Also Gresham Professor of Divinity, Gresham College, London.

Representative Publications

Historical Theology

The Intellectual Origins of the European Reformation. 2nd ed. Oxford: Blackwell, 2003.

Luther's Theology of the Cross: Martin Luther's Theological Breakthrough. 2nd ed. Oxford: Blackwell, 2011.

Iustitia Dei: A History of the Christian Doctrine of Justification. 4th ed. Cambridge: Cambridge University Press, 2020.

Biographies

Thomas F. Torrance: An Intellectual Biography. Edinburgh: T. & T. Clark, 1999.

C. S. Lewis – A Life. Reluctant Prophet, Eccentric Genius. London: Hodder & Stoughton, 2013.

Emil Brunner: A Reappraisal. Oxford: Wiley-Blackwell, 2014.

J. I. Packer: His Life and Thought. London: Hodder & Stoughton, 2020.

Natural Theology

The Open Secret: A New Vision for Natural Theology. Oxford: Blackwell, 2008.

A Fine-Tuned Universe: The Quest for God in Science and Theology. Louisville, KY: Westminster John Knox Press, 2009.

Darwinism and the Divine: Evolutionary Thought and Natural Theology. Oxford: Wiley-Blackwell, 2011.

Re-Imagining Nature: The Promise of a Christian Natural Theology. Oxford: Wiley-Blackwell, 2016.

Science and Religion

A Scientific Theology. 3 vols. Edinburgh: T&T Clark, 2001–2003.

Dawkins' God: Genes, Memes and the Meaning of Life. 2nd ed. Oxford: Blackwell, 2015.

Enriching Our Vision of Reality: Theology and the Natural Sciences in Dialogue. London: SPCK, 2016.

The Territories of Human Reason: Science and Theology in an Age of Multiple Rationalities. Oxford: Oxford University Press, 2019.

Public Engagement: Apologetics

The Dawkins Delusion? Atheist Fundamentalism and the Denial of the Divine. London: SPCK, 2007 (with Joanna Collicutt McGrath).

Mere Apologetics: How to Help Seekers and Skeptics Find Faith. Grand Rapids, MI: Baker Books, 2011.

Narrative Apologetics: Sharing the Relevance, Joy, and Wonder of the Christian Faith. Grand Rapids, MI: Baker Books, 2019.

Theological Textbooks

Christian Theology: An Introduction. 6th ed. Oxford: Wiley-Blackwell, 2016.

The Christian Theology Reader. 5th ed. Oxford: Wiley-Blackwell, 2016.

Theology: The Basics. 4th ed. Oxford: Wiley-Blackwell, 2017.

Reformation Thought: An Introduction. 5th ed. Oxford: Wiley-Blackwell, 2021.

Historical Theology: An Introduction to the History of Christian Thought. 2nd ed. Oxford: Wiley-Blackwell, 2013.

Science and Religion: A New Introduction. 3rd ed. Oxford: Wiley-Blackwell, 2019.